KIDZBIZ

PARTY TIME

Gillian Souter

Off the Shelf Publishing

BEFORE YOU START...

So, you're planning a party! Here are lots of ideas
for making invitations, decorations, games to play,
prizes and things to eat. There are pictures to give
you ideas, but it's fun to make up your own designs
and patterns.

Some of the projects need to be made well before
the party. You might want to make a list of what has
to be done so that it all runs smoothly.

For some projects you might need
an adult's help, especially when you want to use
a sharp knife or to bake something in the oven.

First published in 1999 by
Off the Shelf Publishing
32 Thomas Street
Lewisham NSW 2049
Australia

Projects, text and layout
copyright © 1999 Off the Shelf Publishing
Line illustrations by Clare Watson
Photographs by Andre Martin

Contents

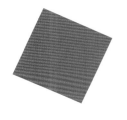

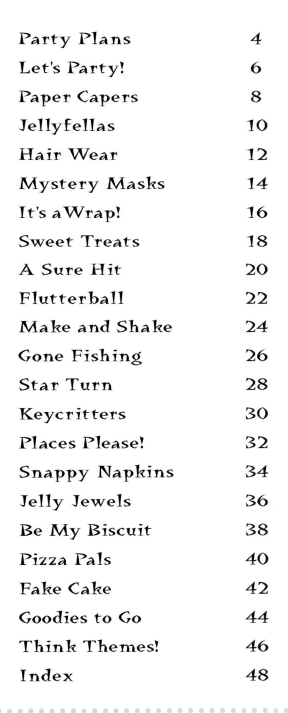

Party Plans

So, you're planning a party. One of the best bits is getting everything ready for it: here are some ideas.

You might want to choose a theme for your party. Look at the ideas at the back of this book and use your imagination to make your party unique.

You'll need to give your friends an invitation which tells them where and when. Also, tell them if you want them to wear something special.

It's easy to decorate a room with streamers and paper chains. Outdoors, you could tie lots of balloons onto branches or fences.

What games will you play at the party? Are there fun things you and your friends could make? Plan all this ahead so it runs smoothly.

You might want to give a small prize to the games winners (or to all your guests). There are ideas for making prizes in this book.

And then there's the food! Make sure that it's not all made of sugar.

You might want to give your friends something nibbly to take home.

Let's Party!

Stencilling is a good way to make lots of invitations with the same design.

YOU WILL NEED

stiff cardboard
scissors
a pencil
a ruler
a craft knife
coloured card
a kitchen sponge
paints
a saucer
a felt pen

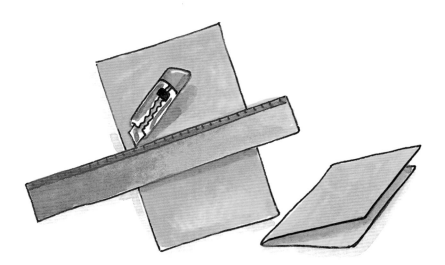

1 Cut rectangles of coloured card. Run a craft knife lightly along the middle of each piece and fold it in half.

2 Cut a piece of stiff cardboard slightly smaller than the front of your invitations. Draw a simple party design on it.

3 Ask an adult to cut out the shapes with a craft knife. Place the stencil over the front of the invitation.

4 Put thick paints on a saucer. Dab a corner of the sponge in one colour and dab it on the design. To change colours, use another corner of the sponge.

5 When the paint is dry, add extra details with a felt pen. You could also add stickers.

Inside the card, write your name, the date and time of the party, where it will be held, and any special information.

7

Paper Capers

Here is a quick way to make bright decorations to hang up in your party room or outdoors.

YOU WILL NEED

crêpe paper
a ruler
a pencil
scissors
glue

1 Draw a line 5 cm from the edge of a roll of crêpe paper and cut along the line. Do the same with another colour of crêpe paper.

2 Glue the ends of the two long crêpe paper strips toegther to make a big 'L' shape.

3 Fold the top strip down and then the side strip across. Keep folding the strips neatly over the centre, one after the other.

4 When you reach the end of a strip, glue the two strips together. Trim off any extra crêpe paper to make the ends neat.

You can make extra long decorations by gluing several chains together.

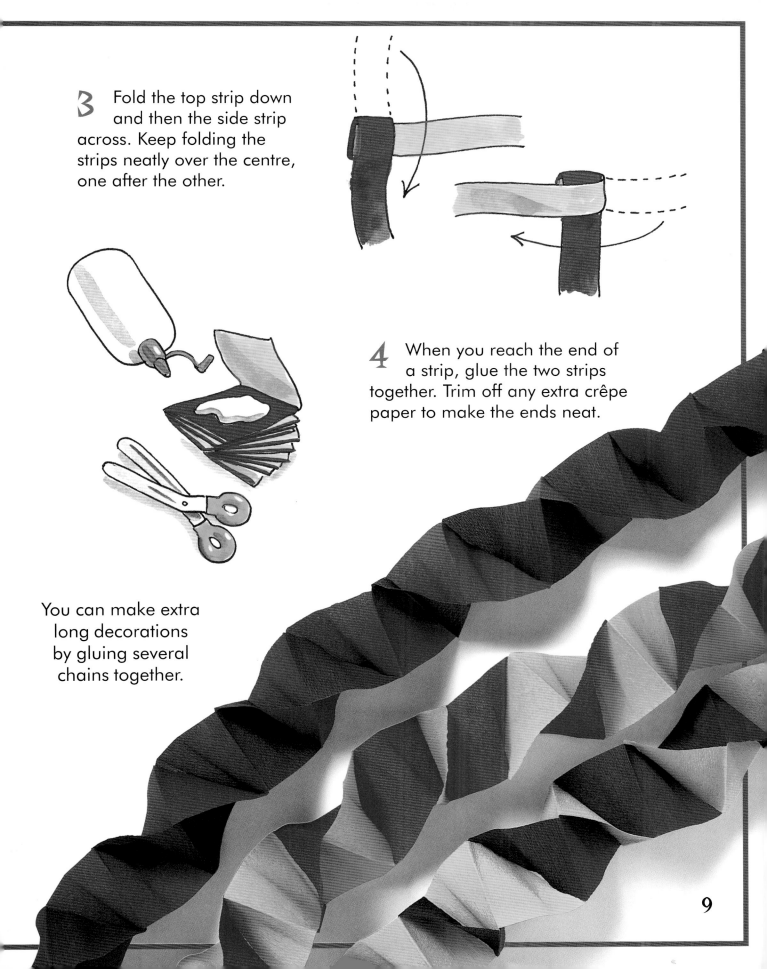

Jellyfellas

A few of these beasties
hanging around will
liven up any party.

1 Cut four or five long
pieces of paper streamer
and punch a hole in one end.

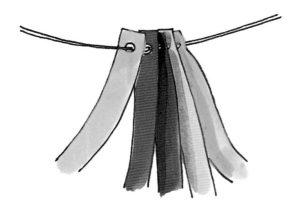

2 Punch two holes in
the base of a plastic
cup with a compass point
or a skewer.

3 Cut a piece of string
and thread it through
the streamers.

4 Thread the string ends
through the holes in
the cup and tie them in an
overhand knot.

5 Draw a face on paper and tape
it inside the plastic cup so that
the face shows through. If you're
using paper cups, draw on the
outside of the cup itself.

Now your jellyfella
is all ready to be
strung up.

Hair Wear

Get all the pieces ready
before the party.
When friends arrive
they can decorate their
own headband.

1 Measure around your head
with a piece of string. Cut
narrow strips of coloured card
a bit longer than the string.
You will need two strips for
each headband.

2 Cut other pieces of card
into feather shapes with
wide stems. Snip each of the
edges towards the middle.

3 Make lots of antennae by
scrunching a piece of foil
around the end of a pipe cleaner.

4 Ask each guest to decorate one card strip with felt pens. Carefully staple feathers or a pair of antennae onto another strip.

5 Lay the two strips together with the feathers in between. Ask an adult to staple the overlapping ends to fit each head.

13

Mystery Masks

Before the party,
prepare the materials
for a cunning disguise
so that your guests
can make their own
as they arrive.

1 Trace over the pattern
at the bottom of this
page, then turn the tracing
over and draw the other
half of the glasses.

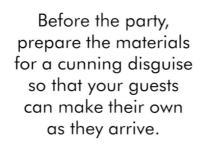

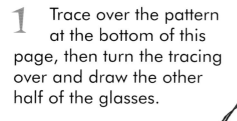

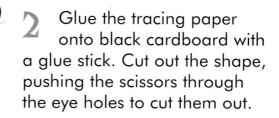

2 Glue the tracing paper
onto black cardboard with
a glue stick. Cut out the shape,
pushing the scissors through
the eye holes to cut them out.

3 Cut up an egg carton and paint the outside of a single cup.

4 Cut a moustache shape from black card. Tape the top of the moustache to the inside of the nose section.

5 Tape the top of the nose section to the back of the glasses. Fold back the arms of the glasses.

You might need to change the length of the arms to fit your head.

It's a Wrap!

Add extra interest to the old game of pass-the-parcel by hiding a paper hat and a 'challenge' in each layer.

1 Measure around your head with a tape measure. Cut wide strips of tissue paper a bit longer than this measurement.

2 Overlap the ends of the strips and glue them together to make a hat. Snip triangles or other shapes from the top edge. Make one hat for each guest.

16

3 Cut the same number of small paper pieces. On each one, write a challenge like: "Pretend you are on a skateboard" or "Sing a song".

4 Wrap up a small prize such as a badge, some stickers, or a small notepad.

5 Keep wrapping the parcel, with a folded paper hat and a challenge in each layer.

Pass the parcel and unwrap a layer each time the music stops. Try to have everyone wearing a hat by the end!

Sweet Treats

Make some dough for
everyone at the party
to model with.
There's one difference:
this dough is edible!

1 Beat the white of an egg
lightly with a fork. Sift in
300 g of icing sugar and mix.
Add a few drops of peppermint
flavour.

2 Knead the mixture until it
is quite smooth. Divide it
into several pieces and put
each piece in a separate bowl.

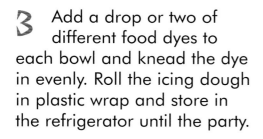

3 Add a drop or two of different food dyes to each bowl and knead the dye in evenly. Roll the icing dough in plastic wrap and store in the refrigerator until the party.

4 Shape the icing dough with clean fingers or with biscuit cutters.

5 Use small sweets to decorate the shapes. Make markings with a fork or a skewer.

The mouse tail is a strip of licorice.

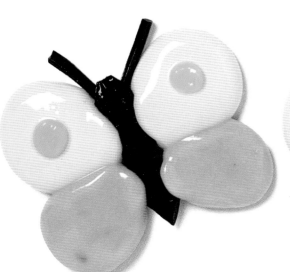

A Sure Hit

Pinatas are made from
papier-mâché for
special occasions in Mexico.
Start making yours a week
before the party.

1   Blow up the balloon to
    the size of a head and
tie a knot. Wipe it all over
with some cooking oil.

2   Mix some PVA glue with the
    same amount of water in a
bowl. Tear some newspaper into
long thin strips. Lay a paper
strip on the balloon and brush
it with paste.

3   Leave the knot of the
    balloon uncovered. Keep
pasting on strips, overlapping
each one. Cover the balloon
with three layers of strips.

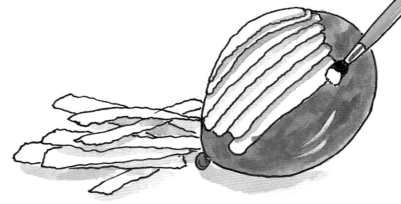

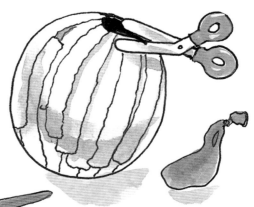

4 Leave the papier-mâché balloon in a dry place for two days. When it is quite dry, prick the balloon with a pin and remove it. Trim the hole at the neck neatly with scissors.

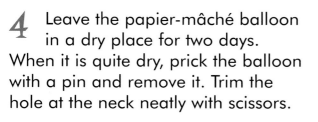

5 Paint the pinata white. When this is dry, paint it in different colours. When the paint is dry, drop in sweets through the hole of the pinata.

6 Ask an adult to make two holes near the neck with sharp scissors. Thread a piece of ribbon through and tie a knot.

Hang the pinata from a tree and take turns to hit at it with a roll of newspaper until it breaks and sweets fly everywhere!

Flutterball

YOU WILL NEED

fabric
a ruler
scissors
an old sock
an elastic band
ribbons

A game of catch is always fun; with this special ball you might even be allowed to play it indoors at the party.

1 Measure and cut a 25 cm square piece of fabric, or use a large handkerchief if you have a spare one.

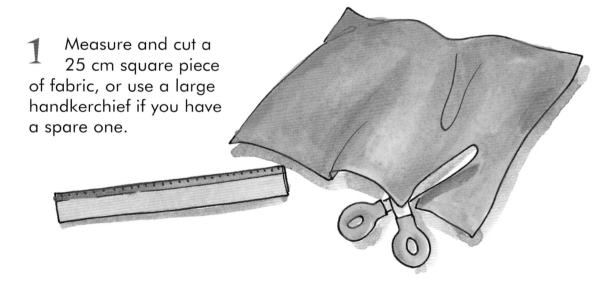

2 Roll an old sock or stocking into a ball and lay it on the fabric square.

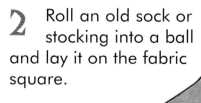

22

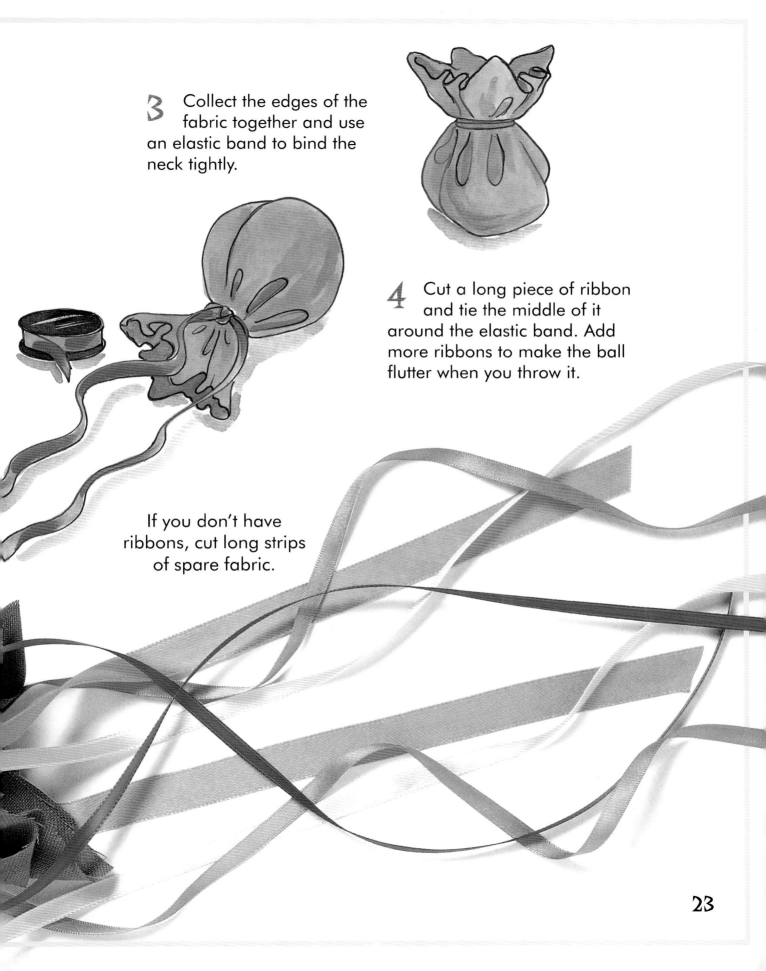

3 Collect the edges of the fabric together and use an elastic band to bind the neck tightly.

4 Cut a long piece of ribbon and tie the middle of it around the elastic band. Add more ribbons to make the ball flutter when you throw it.

If you don't have ribbons, cut long strips of spare fabric.

Make and Shake

Here's a great activity: get everyone to make their own tambourine to play at the party.

YOU WILL NEED

paper plates
tissue paper
curling ribbon
glue
rice
a hole punch

1 Before the party, tear tissue paper into lots of squares and cut long pieces of curling ribbon.

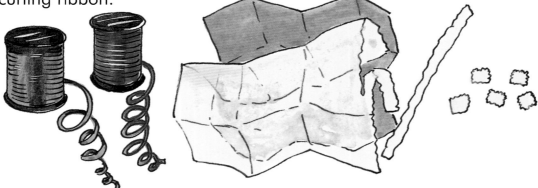

2 Ask each guest to decorate the back of two paper plates by gluing on lots of tissue paper squares.

3 Place a spoonful of uncooked rice on one plate. Spread PVA glue around the raised rim and glue the second plate on top.

24

4 Punch a hole near the edge of the glued plates.

5 Thread the curling ribbons through the hole and pull them half way. Knot the ribbons near the plate.

Make sure the glue has set before you do any serious shaking!

Gone Fishing

Here's a game to make before the party.
Test the length of the ribbon yourself to make sure it's not too easy!

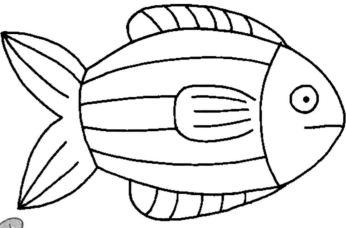

1 Trace over the fish pattern in pencil. Turn the tracing paper over and transfer the design onto coloured card by drawing over the lines.

2 Draw over the pencil lines with a black felt pen.

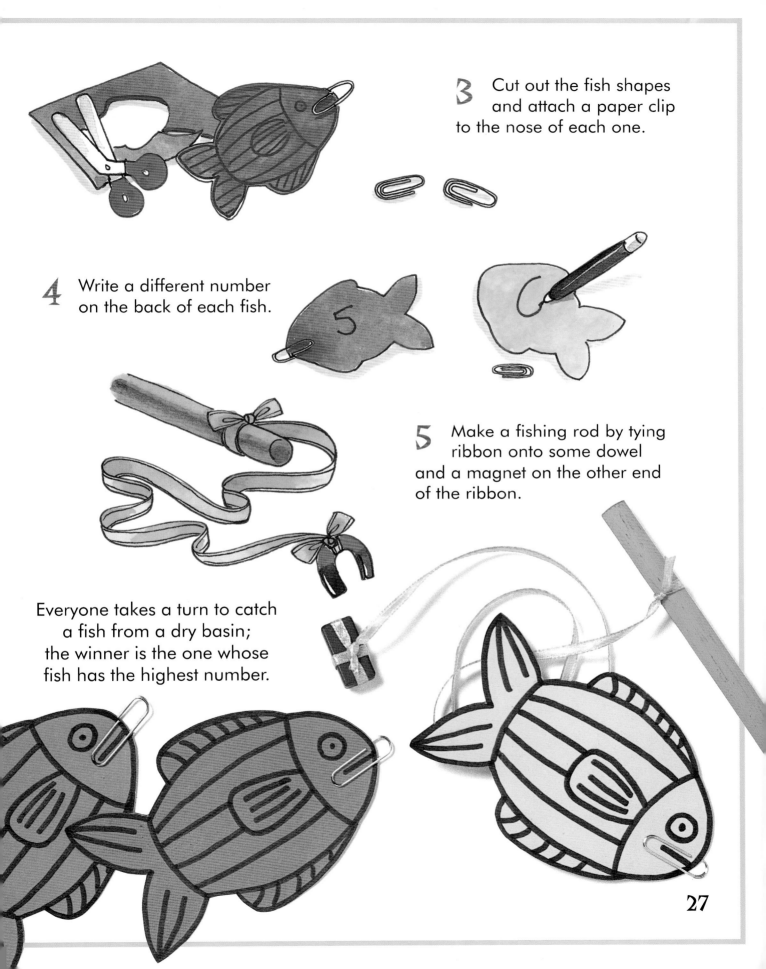

3 Cut out the fish shapes and attach a paper clip to the nose of each one.

4 Write a different number on the back of each fish.

5

5 Make a fishing rod by tying ribbon onto some dowel and a magnet on the other end of the ribbon.

Everyone takes a turn to catch a fish from a dry basin; the winner is the one whose fish has the highest number.

Star Turn

Make some of these bright badges to give as prizes for games at the party.

YOU WILL NEED

tracing paper
a pencil
scissors
pins
coloured felt
pinking shears
a needle
thread
a large safety pin

1 Place tracing paper over the star pattern and draw over it in pencil. Cut out the tracing.

2 Pin the paper star onto a piece of felt and cut around it neatly by snipping inwards.

28

3 Draw a circle around a small lid onto felt and cut it out. On different coloured felt, draw a larger circle around a glass. Cut this out with pinking shears.

4 Thread a needle. Stitch the fixed bar of a large safety pin onto the back of the largest felt shape.

5 Stack the pieces in order of size. Make a couple of stitches through all the layers and tie a knot at the back.

29

Keycritters

Make lots of salt dough keyrings before the party then give them away as prizes.

1   Mix 1/2 cup of plain flour with 1/2 cup of salt in a bowl. Add 1/2 cup of water, a little at a time, and mix until you have a soft dough. Knead this with your hands until the dough is smooth.

If you don't have biscuit cutters, cut shapes from cardboard and cut the dough around them with a knife.

2   Ask and adult to set the oven to 180C/350F/Gas mark 4. Roll out the dough until it is 5 mm thick. Use biscuit cutters to cut interesting shapes from the dough.

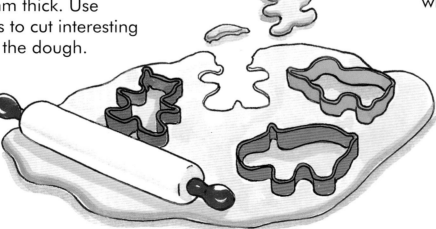

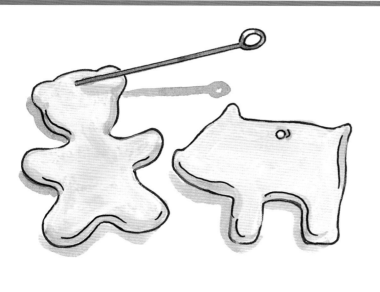

3 Gently place the shapes on an oven tray. Make a hole at the top of each shape with a skewer. Bake them for 2 hours.

4 Let the shapes cool, then paint them in bright colours.

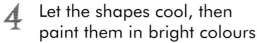

5 Thread a narrow ribbon through the hole and through a keyring. Tie a tight knot and trim the ends.

Try to make sure that each of your friends wins a prize.

Places, Please!

Make an unusual octopus name holder to show each guest where to sit at the party table.

YOU WILL NEED

pipe cleaners
a ruler
scissors
a black pen
PVA glue
thin card

1 Cut two 12 cm pieces of of thick pipe cleaner and lay them flat to make a cross.

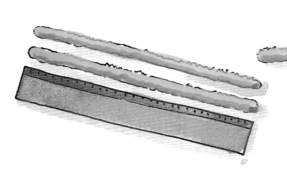

2 Cut an 18 cm length and bind it around the cross to make five equal legs and one very long leg.

3 Bend each piece to make the legs stand. Bend the long leg to make a support for the name card.

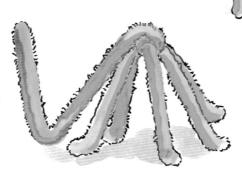

4 Cut another 18 cm length of pipe cleaner and wind it twice around the others to form a head and two extra legs.

5 To make the eyes, draw two small circles on paper and cut them out. Draw a black dot on each circle and glue two eyes on each octopus.

6 Cut a piece of card for each octopus and write a guest's name across the top.

Before the party, arrange the name holders around the table.

33

Snappy Napkins

Printed napkins add a nice touch. If your party has a special theme, think of a suitable design.

1 Draw a shape on a flat kitchen sponge and then cut it out.

2 Glue the sponge shape onto a square of thick cardboard.

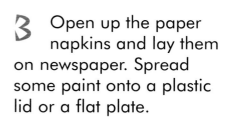

3 Open up the paper napkins and lay them on newspaper. Spread some paint onto a plastic lid or a flat plate.

4 Press the stamp onto the paint and test it on scrap paper. You might need to brush paint onto the sponge to cover it evenly.

5 Press the stamp firmly onto the paper napkin and then lift it up. You may be able to make several prints before the stamp needs more paint.

If your party has a special theme, design a print to suit it.

Jelly Jewels

These jelly quarters look great on the plate and will vanish in seconds. Use the leftover orange pulp for juice or for a dessert.

1 Ask an adult to cut some oranges in half from stem to base.

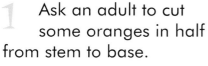

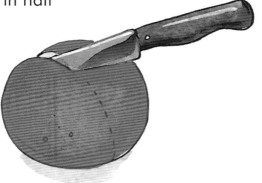

2 Scoop out the pulp from each half-orange and save it in a bowl. Arrange the empty orange cups in a muffin tray.

36

3 Put the jelly crystals in a bowl and add hot water (see the packet for measurements). Stir until all the crystals have dissolved.

4 When the jelly has cooled a little, pour it into the orange cups. Put the tray in the refrigerator.

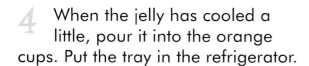

5 When the jelly has set cut each cup in half to make orange quarters. Arrange them on a plate to serve.

Make different flavours and colours for your friends to choose.

Be My Biscuit

Make sure everyone gets an iced cake or biscuit by decorating them with initials or names.

1 Sift 250 g of icing sugar into a bowl. Add 1 tablespoon of warm water and stir the mixture until smooth. Add more water if necessary.

2 Spoon some icing on a biscuit and spread it with the bottom of the spoon. Ice enough biscuits for the party and allow the icing to set.

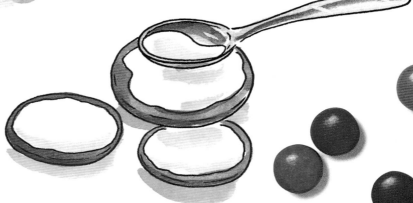

3 Add a few drops of food dye to the remaining icing and stir it in. Put this mixture into a piping bag with a plain nozzle. You can cheat a little by buying coloured icing in a tube!

4 Squeeze the piping bag gently so that icing flows out. Write a letter or name on each biscuit.

5 Pipe some icing around the edge and then stick small sweets onto it.

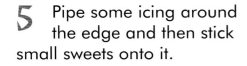

Decorate a few extra biscuits in case you have any unexpected guests.

Pizza Pals

The best pizzas are the ones you make yourself. Get them ready before the party and ask an adult to bake them at the right time.

YOU WILL NEED

1 teaspoon dry yeast
1/2 teaspoon sugar
200g plain flour
1/2 cup warm water
1/4 teaspoon salt
1 tablespoon olive oil
tomato sugo
cheese
toppings
kitchen items

1   Mix the yeast, sugar, 1 teaspoon of flour and warm water in a bowl and leave it for 10 minutes in a warm place. Mix the rest of the flour and salt in another bowl then stir in the yeast mixture and the oil.

2   Knead the dough with your hands for 5 minutes. Put it back in the bowl, cover it and leave it in a warm place for 1 hour or until the dough has doubled in size.

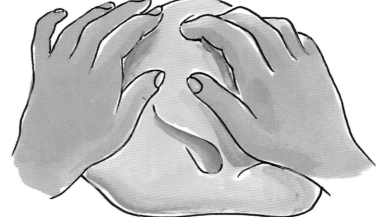

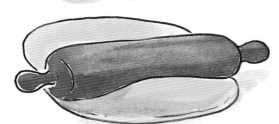

3   Divide the dough into four balls. Roll out each ball until it is a circle 5 mm thick. Place the bases on a greased baking tray.

40

4 Spread tomato sugo (natural tomato sauce) over the base. Grate some cheese and sprinkle it on top.

5 Add the face details with olives, salami, sliced tomato, slivers of capsicum, and so on.

6 Ask an adult to bake the pizzas in an oven preheated to 240C/500F/Gas 7 for 10 to 15 minutes.

This recipe makes four faces so you might need to make twice the amount of dough.

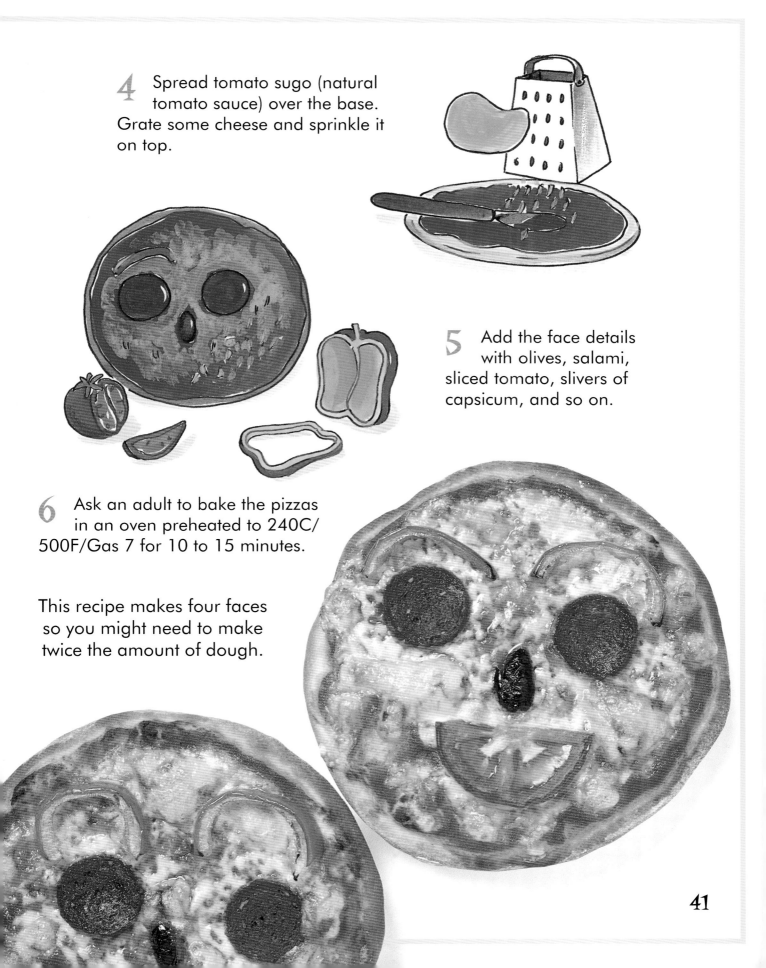

Fake Cake

Some kids like the idea of a cake but don't really like eating it. This cake hides something that all your friends will like!

1 Find a round or square box and remove the lid. Paint the outside of the box white and then a pale colour to look like icing.

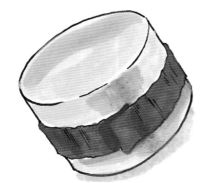

2 Cut a long strip of crêpe paper and wrap it around the box. Glue the overlapping ends.

3 Cut squares of crêpe paper. Fold each square back and forth like a concertina.

4 Wind a thread around the middle and tie a knot. Tweak the ends out to make a butterfly shape. Glue these around the band of crêpe paper.

5 Punch holes in the top of the box with a metal skewer or the point of a compass. Push the candles in.

Now find a bowl that will fit under the box and fill it with sweets.

Goodies to Go

YOU WILL NEED

scrap paper
a piece of string
a pencil
thin card
scissors
strong tape
cellophane
sweets
curling ribbon

Here's something for your guests to take home. You can make shiny cones with foil-covered card or with ready-made party hats.

1 Tie a length of string around a pencil. Hold the other end at the corner of some paper and move the pencil to draw an arc. Cut this out.

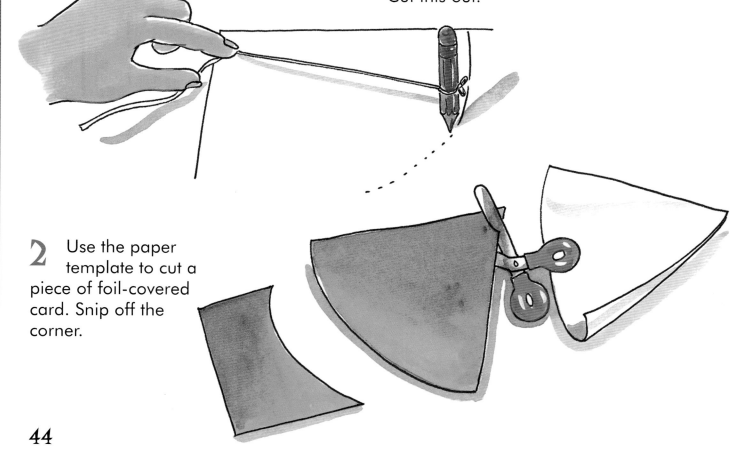

2 Use the paper template to cut a piece of foil-covered card. Snip off the corner.

44

3 Cut a piece of cellophane twice the size of the card. Tape it onto the non-shiny side of the card along each straight edge. Trim the corner of the cellophane.

4 Roll the card into a cone so that the edges overlap. Tape along the edge.

5 Fill the cone with sweets and tie the top with a piece of curling ribbon.

A hint: put some crumpled cellophane in first so sweets don't fall out the bottom!

Think Themes!

Make your party different by choosing a theme and making invitations, decorations, games and food to match.

Red Riot

Ask guests to dress in red, make red decorations, eat strawberries and cherries, and play bobbing for apples. Choose any colour you like!

Out of this World

Use lots of silver foil to decorate your place. Get everyone to make their own antennae. Make a pinata and paint it like planet Earth.

Mermaids & Pirates

Give the party a sea theme
with lots of green seaweed
and cardboard fish. Have a
treasure hunt for gold coins
and play the fishing game.

Monster Meet

Now here's a horrible theme!
Feed your friends green jelly
and weird pizza faces.
Play pin the nose on the ogre.

Teddy Bears' Picnic

Ask guests to bring their
own bear, then give out
prizes for the biggest
ears, the fuzziest fur,
and so on. Serve honey
sandwiches.

Index